My Father

Reflections Through My Christian Life

Clive Jones

First published in Great Britain in 2024

Text and photographic copyright © 2024 Clive Jones

Cover photograph taken from canva.com

Layout, editing & publishing by Andrew Buller - www.andrewbuller.co.uk

All rights reserved. No part of this publication may be reproduced, stored in a retrieval system, or transmitted, in any form or by any means, electronic, mechanical, photocopying, recording or otherwise, without the prior permission of the copyright owner.

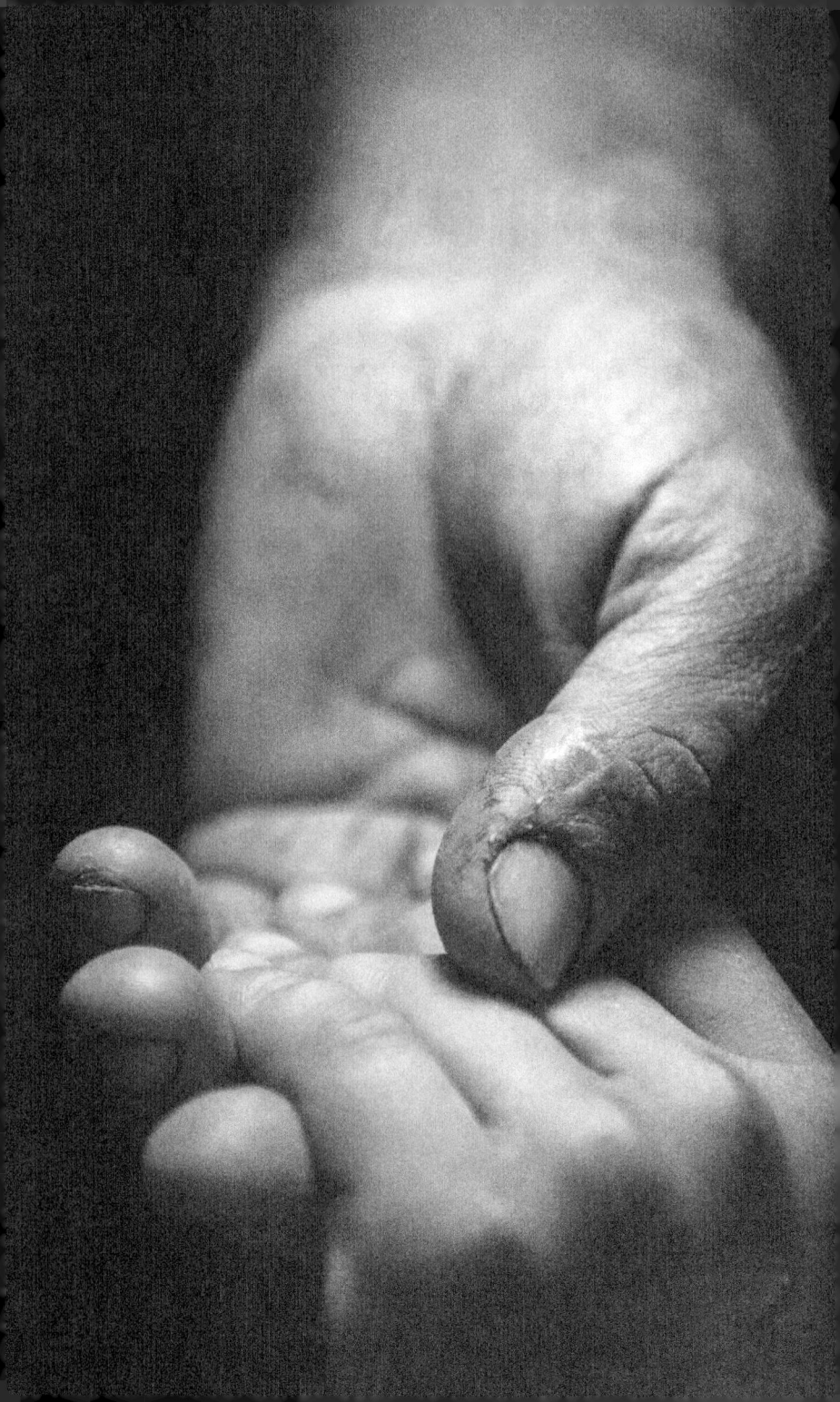

Write these things for the future so that people who are not yet born will praise the LORD. (Psalm 102:18 NCV)

Dedication

This book is dedicated to my strongly supportive wife Lynne, who has always stood by me and encouraged me over the years. She is a faithful friend and a prayerful companion, enabling me to develop in my Christian walk. I would also like to thank those who throughout my life and ministry have imparted the life of Christ to me, exhorting me to trust more and more in my Heavenly Father. From my Sunday school teachers and parents, through to my mentors and prayer partners, I am so grateful for the love, kindness and prayerful support you have afforded me. Thank you all.

My grateful thanks also to Andrew Buller for his expert help in preparing my script for publication.

Preface

In the first week of 2022, I was rushed into hospital very unwell due to three different infections affecting my body after a recent kidney stone removal operation. I was there for seven days, but near the end I was visited by the hospital chaplain, and we had a very pleasant time sharing our journeys of faith with each other. At the end she said to me, Clive you need to write these stories down, as many will be interested to hear of the Lord's working in your life, especially about the "Father heart of God".

Two weeks after my return home we were sharing in a celebration held online on Zoom. The speaker (whom we had never met before) had a prophetic ministry, and spoke into Lynne's and my life at the end of his preach. One of the things he said, that struck me forcibly, was that Lynne and I have many stories to share that should be written down for the benefit of others. Here was a second prompting to write.

Two weeks later, a visiting speaker at our church asked to pray for me knowing I had been unwell, but while asking the Lord for healing he added that I had such a life experience of Jesus that I should write down for the benefit of others, stories of God's ministry into my life. A scripture came to mind, "Let him who has an ear to hear, hear what the Spirit is saying to the churches" (Revelation 2:7).

So here I am, endeavouring to be obedient to the promptings of the Lord and putting down in print, those elements of my life and experience that the Lord has brought to my remembrance. I started more or less straight away but other things crowded in and the manuscript was put onto the back burner. This year, however, I have taken up the challenge once again and am pleased to report it has now been completed.

As I have written, I have been blessed over and over again, as I am overwhelmed yet again by the faithfulness of God. I trust this will be true for the reader who picks up these memories of a life blessed by the Lord. I am so humbled by the Lord's grace poured out in my life. "Thank you, Jesus."

Clive Jones – Staplehurst 2024

My Early Years

I was born in Brighton in April 1947 during one of the most brutal of winters ever known in the UK. Six weeks of snow and blizzard conditions which began in late January led to thousands of people across the country, being cut off in snow drifts. As the UK. was recovering from the effects of the Second World War, the armed forces were deployed to clear roads and railways of snow drifts, some of which were up to seven metres deep. At the end of the big freeze in mid-March, rising temperatures brought a rapid thaw of the deep snow which led to further complications. Meltwaters poured into rivers causing many to burst their banks, adding severe flooding to the immense difficulties the nation had already faced that winter.

My parents, Gwyn and Elsie, together with my sister Phyllis aged five, had recently returned from being incarcerated in a Napoleonic castle in Wurzach, Germany, where they had been held as prisoners of war for two and a half years. My father's father, Edgar Jones, was a Congregational minister. He served for a number of years in a church in Jersey where my father also lived, working as a departmental manager in a store called "Voisins", in St Helier. This store today is proud to be the oldest family run departmental store in Britain, having been launched in 1837.

"Voisons" today in King Street, St Helier, Jersey

My parents met in Brighton and married in 1938 at Lewes Road Congregational Church, but moved to Jersey to live, where my sister, Phyllis was born in 1940.

Clive's parents Gwyn and Elsie Jones

During the war, the German army occupied the Channel Islands, and although many British born people were able to escape back to the mainland, my family were among those unable to do so. With over 600 other people from Jersey, my family, including Phyllis who was only two and a half, were taken as prisoners of war to Germany, only being repatriated in 1945, and able to return to Britain at the end of the war. The "Voisins" company was only able, due to the privations of the aftermath of war, to offer dad his old job back for two days a week, the income from which was insufficient to support the family. So they moved to Brighton, where mum's family lived and were later given a flat in Kemp Town by Brighton Council from whom dad had procured a job. Here I was born.

Interestingly, despite the difficulties caused as a result of the German occupation, friendships were forged between the towns of Wurzach and St Helier, the capital of Jersey, and a formal twinning between the two towns was eventually made. Here perhaps, a pointer to the vital need for forgiveness and reconciliation in all of our lives, no matter how traumatic our past history.

I was able in 1961, as my parents returned to Jersey for the first time since the war, to visit a variety of their friends and neighbours, and to get a flavour of those early days of their married lives before the occupation. I remember the excitement I felt as mum and dad showed me round their special places on the island, and it was a joy for me later in my married life to visit with my wife, Lynne, some of those places again. We were privileged to have a couple of holidays in Jersey, staying in a Christian hotel near La Corbiere Lighthouse.

When I was three, my family were offered a new council house, built on the outskirts of Brighton on an estate called Coldean, where I spent the rest of my school age years attending Coldean Primary, and Stanmer Secondary schools.

My final year at Coldean primary School 1958 with my teacher Mr Bowyer. I am sat on the wall fourth to the right of Mr Bowyer.

I didn't pass my 11+ exam so went to Stanmer Secondary school which was within walking distance through Stanmer Woods. What happy memories both my sister and I have of playing in those woods, as well as Stanmer Park itself. I enjoyed my time at senior school, though I was pleased when I finished studying at school having obtained four "O" levels, in English language, English literature, Geography and Woodwork.

Stanmer Secondary School 1958-1963

I have many happy memories of those years and though our income was fairly low, mum and dad always managed to give us happy holidays, purchasing a family runabout ticket on the railways opening up the south coast from Brighton to Rye. We walked from home to Falmer Station catching the train to Eastbourne, Bexhill, Hastings and Rye, amongst other destinations, finishing the days with a real treat for Phyllis and I - beans on toast and a knickerbocker glory! At other times we stayed with family in Halstead, Essex, where dad's parents lived out their last days, and in Peterborough, where mum's sister Phyllis, her husband Lionel and their daughter Cheryl lived. Both these families were Christians and had profound influences on my fledgling Christian faith.

I have become very conscious, in my later life, of the prayers prayed over me by family and friends over many years, for the Lord Jesus to reveal Himself to me personally. I remember one of my Sunday school teachers, who attended my ordination service, telling me she had prayed for me from my childhood when I had been in her class! I was quite a handful in those days, I remember.

The picture above is one of four generations of my family on my father's side, taken in 1913, when my dad was 18 months old. His father Edgar is to dad's left. Dad is being held by his mother, Annie (nee Harrod). In the front row, from left to right are Henry Jones, my great, great grandad, great grandma Ann (nee Evans), holding my dad's elder sister Myfanwy, and great grandad William Jones. The Lord reminded me at one stage that all these were of a Christian heritage and no doubt prayed for me even before I was born. What a great heritage in Christ I have. Praise the Lord! God my Father was looking after me even before I was born.

My parents attended Union Church Brighton, a central Congregational church, in the town, which later became known as Brighton Central Free Church and more recently "Brighthelm".

They attended this church from their return to Brighton and dad became firstly a deacon, then an elder in this congregation. Mum and dad's faith was very real, but private, and because it was personal, it was hardly ever talked about. However, I was regularly taken each week to Sunday school, church services and later by my own volition to the youth group which met on Sunday evenings after church.

I was a believer all throughout my upbringing and never doubted the existence of God. But my understanding was purely head knowledge, and I had no real comprehension of a personal relationship with Jesus.

Yet, through it all, my relationship with my dad was close and I was later to tell him, once the Lord had revealed Himself to me, that dad had given to me an example of what I could experience, in a much greater measure of course, from the Father heart of God. This was to prove most helpful in later ministry as I discovered that many people have a poor understanding of their relationship with God as Father because of bad, poor or non-relationships with their earthly fathers. I was fortunate to have had a good example in my father. "Thank you, Lord".

At one stage, later in life during my ministry in New Malden, I felt to write to my parents thanking them for the way they had brought me up, and sharing with them my testimony of what Jesus had meant to me since becoming a Christian. I expressed my strong desire to know that we would stand together in the presence of the Lord forever. It always seemed so difficult to talk these things through face to face, and having watched a film series entitled "Focus on the Family" by Dr James Dobson, in which he talked about his relationship with his father and how it seemed appropriate to write to him to share deeply personal things about their relationship with Jesus, I took up a similar prompting and wrote a letter. I share my dad's hand written reply below, which is still a rich treasure to me:

15.04.1985. Dear Clive, I have just this minute put down your letter you felt moved by recent events to write to us. We are both very moved by your expressed sentiments, of which of course we were already aware in no small degree, as you have never been backward in expressing your feelings to us. This has always been a joy to us, but of course one can never hear it expressed too often. We both hope that you do not feel disappointed that we have neither of us felt moved to embrace your evangelical approach to our expression of our love of our Lord and His Son Jesus Christ. I feel, and no doubt your mother does too, that we must all be left to express our feelings in our own individual way. You have your own way (and we glory in it) and we, of an older generation, have ours. We both have been aware of your reasons for opening up your heart and life to Jesus since your decision to do so many years back, although we may not have discussed it, but I personally have always believed that such decisions must come from within to be of lasting conviction and not as a result of mass hysteria. This is why I never insisted that you or Phyllis should go to church, but rather introduce you to reasons as to why you should want to go of your own free will. It might seem a bit haphazard to you, but at least you were in the right place at the right time to receive God's message and call to service. We must not judge the rights and wrongs of the various approaches of various sections of the church, so long as we are all united in the one desire to win people to the acceptance of Christ in their lives. Both your mum and I are still doing our small bit toward the furtherance of His kingdom by our service as our health permits in our various ways, as we have done over our married lives, and before. No doubt we could have done better, and more, but we pray for forgiveness for our sins of omission and commission. We both trust that you have no doubt of our love for you and yours, for as parents, we should have borne this love however you had lived your life, but we give thanks and pray for worthiness for the gift of a son who has turned out as you have. God bless you and keep you.

Tons and tons of love. Yours as ever, Mum and Dad.

Having received and read that letter I knew my parents were united with Lynne and myself in a living relationship with Jesus. What a wonderful answer to prayer!

I have a vivid memory, etched in my mind, of a time when I was 18 years old, singing a hymn during an evening service, when I heard a voice clearly say to me, "I want you to serve me full-time". The voice was so clear I looked behind me to see who had spoken it to me, but there was just another member singing their heart out. I said to my then girlfriend afterwards, "I think God spoke to me in that service". However, she was not impressed, saying something along the lines of, "God does not speak to people like that today". Because I did not really have a personal relationship with Jesus at the time I put the matter to the back of my mind. But God does not forget!

Coming To Faith In Christ

Being a part of the youth group in the church (our congregation was about 300 at the time) we were invited to take services to help some of the small village churches around Sussex. I had the opportunity to lead services and sometimes preach, and was even asked to speak for a session at a youth conference held at Ashburnham Place in Sussex. All this as a believer, without any personal relationship with Jesus. How amazing is the Lord who is constantly at work behind the scenes working out His purposes for our lives. In retrospect, it is gratifying to realise just how much the Lord's hand was upon me as I grew up, even without any acknowledgement of Him on my part.

By 1967, I had become the chairman of the church youth group which met on Sunday evenings after church. I was asked by one of the young ladies in the group, Lynne (incidentally now my wife since 1969) if we could invite a speaker from "Campus Crusade for Christ" to share with our group. They had recently sent a contingent of young evangelists from America to Brighton, to minister to students in the colleges of the town and Sussex University. Lynne had met them at Falmer, her college where she was training to be a teacher, and through sharing a survey and convicting conversation, they had enabled her to discover Jesus for herself, and begin a journey of faith with Him.

I was somewhat wary of such an invitation but could not think of any reason to say no. So it was that Charlie, together with another member of the team, Shari, came along to talk to our group which numbered about 25 that evening. They talked in such a way about their relationship with Jesus that was so real, and to me, mind-blowing, for I had never heard anyone talk in such a personal way about their faith and relationship with Jesus. Shari even testified to her mother having been healed by Jesus! I was so excited about what I heard, that I longed for such a relationship with Jesus for myself. As we closed the meeting, I asked Charlie if I might close in prayer. I asked Jesus to forgive me and to come into my life and the lives of all those gathered there that evening. For the first time in my life, I opened up my heart to Jesus and He came flooding in.

As Charlie had pointed out, "If you think you are Christian because your parents are, or because you believe in God, or you go to church, or you do good deeds or have been baptised, you are very much mistaken. You only become a Christian, as you acknowledge your need of Christ's forgiveness for the sin in your life, that He died in your place on the cross of Calvary, and ask Him to come into your life to begin the work of regeneration."

Here began a life of adventure with Jesus that has pervaded the whole of the rest of my life. I remember Phyllis, my sister asking me at one point, "Are you afraid of dying?" Certainly, I had been in my teenage years, sometimes even fearing the future should my parents die young. Yet having been asked the question, I realised that this particular fear had been lifted from me. I later found great assurance in a verse from Hebrews 2:14-15 which confirmed this. "Since the children [You and I] have flesh and blood, he too [that is, Jesus] shared in their humanity so that by his death he might destroy him who holds the power of death – that is, the devil – and free those who all their lives were held in slavery by their fear of death." I had been fearful, but now imperceptibly, He had set me free. Hallelujah!

Lynne and I started a prayer and Bible study together for our youth group, and for several weeks we were the only two in attendance, but gradually others began to come and we saw many lives changed as we put our trust in Jesus, asking the Holy Spirit to lead us.

It was during this time that Lynne read the book, "The Cross and the Switchblade" by David Wilkerson, which tells of the godly transformations amongst the gang culture in America. Here she read of the baptism of the Holy Spirit and how God's power changed gang member's lives, setting them free from drugs and wrong living. Her response was to fall to her knees in her bedroom at college (she had a room overlooking the seafront at Eastern Terrace in Brighton) asking the Lord to baptise her in the Holy Spirit, saying, "I won't move from here until it happens". The Lord honoured her heart cry. However, this did cause a hiccup in our relationship for a while because my pride came to the fore and I felt quite peeved saying, "What's so special about you? Why does God not do this for me?"

Fortunately, a few weeks later in one of our Bible study/prayer sessions in which we looked at the ministry of the Holy Spirit in both Old and New Testaments, the Lord graciously baptised me in the Holy Spirit too, and what a change He began to formulate in my life! I often describe my Christian experience up until this point as like sitting in a theatre with the orchestra playing the overture, when suddenly (as the Holy Spirit comes) the curtains open and a whole new world is revealed as stage lights reveal actors and staging that are mesmerising.

I love the description of one of the Puritan Fathers, Thomas Goodwin, as he endeavours to explain the experience of the Baptism of the Holy Spirit. A father and son are walking along together holding hands, very much aware of their mutual love for one another, when suddenly the father looks down at his son and in an overwhelming moment of passion picks up his son in a strong loving embrace and says, "I do so love you", and the son responds with his affirmation of love as well. For Thomas this exemplified his understanding of the increased and deeper love relationship with the Lord when he experienced baptism in the Holy Spirit. This experience, linked with the understanding of the good relationship I had with my earthly father, opened up an ever-deepening relationship with God as my Father.

First Steps In Evangelism

Campus Crusade helped to disciple us in those early days, teaching us through the Scriptures, using a booklet entitled "The Four Spiritual Laws". It taught us the importance of prayer and encouraged us to share our faith with others.

A discipleship meeting with Charlie second from right and myself top right, 1969

One significant experience of sharing the good news of Jesus comes to mind. I was taken by a member of the Campus Crusade team onto Brighton Seafront to talk to others about my faith. At one point, as we walked along the promenade, we were stopped by a gentleman we didn't know, who pointed us towards a person sitting down on the beach. "That person needs to know about the Lord. Go and talk to him." We immediately went to speak to them, but suddenly thought, "Why didn't he go himself if he was aware of this fact?" However, he had disappeared by this time. In the discussion that followed we thought maybe we had experienced an encounter with an angelic being! In sharing with the man on the beach, I was able to testify to my new found faith and within a short time we were able to pray together as he invited Christ into his life.

Lynne and I continued sharing our faith as we had been encouraged, and spent many evenings visiting the "Archway Project" on Brighton seafront. A group of hippies and young people, many of whom were drug addicts, had been given several enclosed archways under the promenade by the Council to gather and spend time with one another. Lynne and I endeavoured to draw alongside these hurting and broken people, sharing how much we believed they were loved by God. Some believed and shared their experiences of the Lord, but so often their brokenness overwhelmed them. Some even captured their experiences of life in poetry.

I remember one young man who had come from a good background but had felt rejected by his parents. Every time he longed to get alongside them, be accepted by them, and spend time with them, all they did was to give him money and told him to go off and have a good time. He had been drawn into the drug culture because here he felt accepted and loved by those around him in the archway. This really saddened me, and made me so grateful for the loving family life I had experienced growing up.

I met with Charlie once a week in those early days of my Christian Walk. He came to meet with me in my lunch hour at the place of my employment. I did not know what to do when I left school and my dad introduced me to the chief technician in the technical college where he worked as a janitor. As a result, I was offered a job and worked as a laboratory technician from when I left school at age 16, in the Pharmacy department of Brighton College of Technology. I worked in several different labs including Pharmaceutical Chemistry, Microbiology and the Dispensary.

I studied on day release for five years at Brighton technical College for a qualification of the City and Guilds in advanced chemistry, which I thankfully accomplished enabling me to obtain a senior lab technicians post. I discovered other Christians in the college and joined the student Christian Union that met at lunchtimes too. It was here that I learnt how to pray with others in a group, in what they called a "chain prayer"! One person started, then each in the circle prayed one after another. I thought what shall I pray about? I settled in my mind a subject then found someone else prayed the same thing. I panicked, getting hot under the collar, until in the end my turn came and went and I had managed my first chain prayer meeting. Thank you, Lord!

Brighton College of Technology -
I worked on the top floor

Thank you, Lord indeed! One of those students Nigel Spencer, felt called to join Campus Crusade at the time and has been involved, with his wife Helene, in Christian evangelistic/teaching ministry in Europe ever since. I am still in touch today via Facebook.

Nigel Spencer in 2016

One day, one of the Campus Crusade team met me at lunchtime at college, instead of Charlie. Apparently, Charlie had received his call up papers for the American army to go fight in Vietnam, and had to return to the States to sort out legally his desire to stay involved in Christian ministry rather than join the army. I felt bereft! I had been depending on Charlie to help me in my Christian journey and now he was gone. The Lord had to teach me through this experience just how vital it is to build one's own personal relationship with Jesus, grateful for other people's input, but not relying on them. I needed to fully cast myself upon the Lord for my daily walk. This was an excellent lesson to learn in order that I could encourage others to trust their lives completely into the Lord's hands, rather than being strongly influenced by charismatic personalities that we might meet, who could easily let us down or disappoint us.

Love In The Air!

My relationship with Lynne developed from a platonic friendship into a growing, loving relationship. When she returned back to her home in Castle Bromwich during the college summer vacations, I found myself really missing her. We kept in touch by writing to one another most days, and then while I was on holiday with my parents, visiting my sister, and Lynne on holiday with hers, I felt called to travel to Padstow in Cornwall where they were staying.

Within minutes of meeting up again we held hands for the first time, and something akin to an electric shock went through me. I was in love!

Within eleven months of going out together we felt the Lord leading us to get married. I popped the question one night, a proposal of marriage, but Lynne's reply caught me by surprise. Instead of saying yes, she replied that she would pray about it and let me know. The wind was taken right out of my sails, but not too many days later she came back with an affirmative reply! Praise the Lord! Another lesson taught, of the need to commit our plans to the Lord for checking out just what

He thinks. Or perhaps, more importantly, seeking His plans rather than ours!

As we were discussing our future plans together, the Lord's words spoken into my heart when I was eighteen, three years earlier, came flooding back into my mind, "I want you to serve me full-time". We made an appointment to see our minister, the Rev. P. Gwyn Filby, and he talked through with us the possibilities that we might follow. It was as our pastor spoke of training to be a minister of the Gospel that my heart leapt, and I knew what the Lord was asking of me.

Lynne and I felt it right to investigate the possibility of training for the ministry, and so our minister set the ball rolling for the training process to begin within the Congregational denomination. I needed to go through a series of interviews in order to test out my calling. On one weekend conference I met a fellow interviewee, somewhat older than me, who was also being interviewed for a role as a church minister. His name was Garth Moody from New Zealand, and we really jelled together, as we were on a similar wavelength, spiritually speaking.

This relationship was truly the provision of the Lord. Many years later, while I was seeking a church to pastor after completing my college training, Garth, then ministering in Wimbledon, at Dundonald Congregational Church, was also the moderator advising the church in New Malden where I was, a few years later, to begin my ministry. He put my name forward as a possible candidate and the rest is history!

Marriage

Lynne and I married in August 1969 at my home church, Union Church, Queen's Square in Brighton, the service being conducted by our minister, Gwyn Philby. Lynne, having graduated with a teaching diploma from Sussex University, looked for a job near the college where I would start my training at New College, London University in Hampstead.

Lynne and Clive's wedding, 2nd August 1969
at Union Church, Brighton

The Lord amazingly provided her a teaching post at Parliament Hill girl's school, a few miles away from the college, as a Maths/R.E. teacher. On the same day as her interview, she met in the staff room a lady who lived in a flat in Kentish Town, a short walking distance from the school, who was emigrating to Canada on the day we were getting married. Lynne went and spoke with the landlady of that flat, before returning to Brighton, who also happened to be a Mrs Jones, a Welsh lady who attended the Welsh Church in London. As a result, Lynne came back to Brighton having been offered a job and procured accommodation on the same day! What a wonderful provision of the Lord! He was certainly on our case. Our Father was looking after us indeed!

I too saw God's provision of a job lasting for a year before I was due to start my training in September 1970. Some years previously, one of my colleagues in the Pharmacy department in Brighton, Ray Mitchell, had moved to a new job at Westfield College, just across the road in Hampstead from the college I was due to train in. I wrote and asked if he had any vacancies in his department, which he did, and I was offered a post in the Botany department of that college working alongside a professor, Dr Peter Fay, who was studying and researching the life cycle of algae. I became his technician to set up the experiments he wanted to carry out.

Charlie and Clive in 2017 at St Helen's, Bishopsgate

So it was, that having married, we moved into the flat in Kentish Town where we remained for five years, while I worked at Westfield College for that first year, before starting my four-year ministry training course at New College. Charlie, had by this time, sorted out his army draft papers and was released to continue in Christian ministry. He returned to the UK and having learnt of my decision to train in a Congregational college, the denomination I had grown up in, pleaded with me to re-consider my plans, suggesting I might attend an evangelical Bible college instead. He was concerned, I think, that I would receive liberal teaching and have my faith knocked out of me. He elicited a promise from me to pray and reconsider, but the Lord only reaffirmed for me the existing course of action to train at New College.

Fortunately, Charlie's fears were not realised, for the opposite became true, as I became more and more deeply grounded in my faith. I still saw Charlie several times while he remained in the UK but his calling took him elsewhere and although today, he is still in Christian ministry in various places around the world, we regularly communicate with one another, and have seen one another two or three times in the last 50 years. I have been so grateful for his prayerful interest in my life and ministry, and am eternally grateful that he took time to help me discover a living relationship with the Lord Jesus Christ.

Lynne worked solidly at Parliament Hill girl's school, and became second in the maths department, while establishing, with an evangelical Anglican lady, Heather, and a Catholic nun, Teresa, a very lively Christian Union for the girls, a number of whom became Christians themselves during that period. I was privileged to speak at their Christian Union several times over the five years Lynne taught at that school. They even were able to organise an after-school concert with "The Forerunners", a gospel group touring the UK, from Campus Crusade. An appeal was given at the end of the concert and several girls came forward to receive Christ. Many of those who came to faith during Lynne's time at the school are still going on with the Lord, and some keep in touch with us still, 50 years later.

There was one time, a few years ago, when Lynne was going through a particularly tough time at the school she was teaching at in Kent, when out of the blue we received a letter and photograph from a dozen of the girls we used to help in those early years in Kentish Town. Apparently, they still meet together from time to time and felt to write a letter to Lynne. They said they didn't think they had ever said thank you for leading them to Christ through the Christian Union and our home Bible studies, so they wanted to do so now.

That was such an uplift for Lynne and a great encouragement to us both. You see, we had set up a Bible study in our home for those girls on a Sunday afternoon and travelled with them afterwards on a number 27 bus from Kentish Town to Notting Hill Gate where we attended, "Kensington Temple", an Elim Pentecostal church. The time we spent there, under the ministries of Eldin Corsie and Lyndon Bowring, was very formative in our developing Christian faith and experience, as well as for those young ladies.

Lynne and I very often on Friday nights would join an evangelistic team sharing the good news of Jesus with people on the streets of Notting Hill. We would meet at 10pm for prayer and then go out onto the streets to talk and share testimony with the many people around at that time of night, perhaps till about two o'clock in the morning. We obviously were pleased to have a lie in on Saturday mornings after such an exciting evening before. We had some really good conversations and opportunities to pray with people, although at times we were mocked for our faith and even once, an aggressive person chose to spit in my face.

Lynne did teach "A" Level R.E. to a couple of girls in her first year of teaching. One, a very lively young lady, Glenys, with an extrovert character, came from a Salvation Army background and was very outspoken about her faith. She even asked Lynne in one of her first teaching sessions if she was saved!

The other girl was much quieter and came from a Quaker background. Elizabeth, the Quaker, knew about God, but had no personal relationship with Him and we had the privilege of talking to her about how the Lord had revealed Himself to us. She too joined us on some of those Sunday afternoon Bible studies.

Elizabeth was extremely intelligent and went on to do classics at Cambridge University where wonderfully, in her first term, she wrote to tell us she had invited Christ into her life. I remember her excitedly telling us of an experience she and the whole group of the Christian Union she had joined. Apparently, they had been in prayer for some time when all of a sudden, they corporately began crying and sobbing uncontrollably. This lasted for some time. When they finished, a prophetic message was given, informing them that they had carried in prayer the pain of the suffering a persecuted believer had undergone, and their prayer had enabled that believer to stand strong. What amazing things can happen to us as we devote our lives to serve our Lord unreservedly!

After graduation, Elizabeth went on to work with the Wycliffe Bible Translators and spent over 25 years working in northern Cameroon translating the New Testament into the Podoko language.

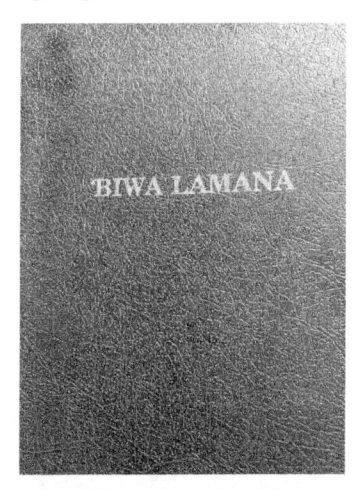

Cover of Podoko New Testament

I am privileged to have a copy of that Bible in my study which was published in 1992. She visited us several times and spoke a couple of times in my first church in New Malden. Having completed that translation, we were saddened to hear the news that Elizabeth had contracted cancer and she died a premature death at age 54. She had certainly served her Lord well, gained her reward, and entered the eternal presence of the One she loved and adored.

Ministerial Training

Starting full-time studies for me at college in 1970 proved to be quite tough. I had left school in 1963, and although I had completed day release part-time education to obtain City and Guilds in Advanced Chemistry to qualify me to improve my work status as a senior laboratory technician, this theological study proved something else! I had to work so hard to keep up, particularly with Greek and Hebrew.

New College, Hampstead, London 1970-74 - second row down, fourth from left with beard!

All the time in lectures I was hearing teaching, and as I contemplated what I heard, I was asking myself did I believe this, or was the teaching I received via Campus Crusade and my conservative evangelical commentaries and dictionaries, more believable? This was both stimulating and a challenge.

My first lecture in the college was in Christian Doctrine where the Principal, Dr Duthie spent an hour basically saying that in the 1970s one could no longer hold a Biblical doctrine of Creation. At the close of his lecture, I had to make a speedy decision, and when asked for questions and comments, I said that I totally refuted all that Dr Duthie had shared because I **did** hold a Biblical view of Creation. (How audacious of me!) Both he and the other students turned on me, trying to point out from their perspective, how foolish I was to hold that position.

One of the students came to me the very next day and apologised that he had not stood with me, because he agreed with my perspective, but was afraid to speak out, and later that term, he left to join another college. I have to say, with a twinkle in my eye, that every year after that, Dr Duthie put a question in the Christian doctrine exam paper about the doctrine of Creation and I answered in the same way each time. After my last exam was returned to me, a comment was written by the principal saying, "Oh, Clive, will you never learn?"

Though study did not come easy for me, I did at last accomplish passing my academic diploma in theology of London University, but I was more keen on being involved in people's lives rather than study. I thoroughly enjoyed a student pastorate in East Ham Presbyterian church in my second year, with a longer involvement with Haringey United Church in my final year.

Before Lynne and I got married we had both been convicted of the need to be baptised by total immersion as believers, but because I was to train in a denomination that in general did not practise believers' baptism, I was persuaded by others to put it off. However, I do believe that our spiritual growth became somewhat stunted as a result because we were putting off, what we had become convinced, was a command from our heavenly Father and the Lord Jesus. When I discovered that the church in Haringey had its own baptistery, I went to see the principal and shared my dilemma. "Don't let it be a problem to you Clive. I was baptised in the sea when I was eighteen," was his reply.

Without further ado, Lynne and I made arrangements with the minister, Rev Jim Hammond, at Haringey, and were duly baptised in my final year at college. Can I say, from my experience, blessing always follows being obedient to Christ.

We learnt a lesson about giving and trusting the Lord while we were at Haringey. At one point in the year, we were challenged by the speaker to give 1% of our finances to Christian Aid. Lynne's salary at that time was just over £900 per year so 1% equated to around £10. That was all we had in the bank at the time, plus a few pounds in our purse to see us through the week with food. We looked at one another and felt it right to write a cheque and give those ten pounds.

The next day, Monday, we had a letter from friends posted on Friday saying the Lord had told them to send a gift of one hundred pounds to support us. How amazing! We mused as we prayed and gave thanks, contemplating how we might have felt receiving that money, if we hadn't given away ten pounds the day before. We were so glad we listened to those inner promptings and so grateful to the Lord for His provision and the lesson learnt, to trust Him continually for His provision. God is a generous Father and He wanted us to be generous too.

As a college we held an evangelistic mission in the Haringey church in 1973, and worked as a team throughout the week of mission in various meetings and open-air ministry. One of the meetings was a film night and I was deputised to collect the film "Two A Penny" starring Cliff Richard from the Billy Graham Evangelistic Association H.Q. in Camden Town. As I got into the lift to go to the desired floor to collect the film, who should step inside at that very moment, but Billy Graham himself. This was the one and only time I ever met him personally, but we had a great conversation, and I was able to thank him for his amazing ministry in sharing the good news of Jesus around the world. During more than 60 years of public ministry, he preached the Gospel of Christ in person, to more than 80 million people and saw approximately 3 million people respond to the invitations he gave at the end of his sermons. What an amazing statistic!

I was privileged to give the closing evangelistic address at the end of the mission. Dr Duthie our principal came along as well. I saw him taking notes, as was his practise in sermon class at college and I wondered what criticism he might give me. At the end two people came forward to give their lives to Christ and I saw Dr Duthie tear up his notes. Afterwards he said he was indeed picking up various critical points to share with me later, but as he realised people were moved to give their lives to the Lord, he felt criticism was not appropriate. The Lord had overruled any failings on my part!

During my time training at college many discussions took place between the Congregational Church and the Presbyterian Church about coming together as one, and in 1973 the union came about with the United Reformed Church being established. This proved somewhat difficult for me for I was told by the first moderator of the URC that there was no place for me within the new denomination, unless I was prepared to baptise infants. With my understanding on believer's baptism and the personal struggles I had already gone through, I now had to make a decision. Do I subscribe to the dictates of the URC or do I leave the denomination? I had been a part of that church for 27 years of my life!

I chose to leave and had to cast myself upon the Lord for His direction and help. Three churches were brought to my attention, one in Scotland, one in the east end of London and one in New Malden, Surrey.

I preached in all three but had no idea of where the Lord would have me go, until one day in prayer, the Lord spoke very clearly to me, as though a human voice was in the room, "You are my man for New Malden".

I was at home in the flat by myself at the time but felt I needed to go into college to share with one of my dear friends, Richard, what I felt the Lord had said to me. There is power in agreement and he prayed with me. When the invitation to become the minister in New Malden came from their leadership and church meeting, I already had the answer to reply with.

Thus, in September 1974 I was ordained and inducted to the pastorate of New Malden Evangelical church, affiliated to the Fellowship of Independent Evangelical churches, and affectionately known as "Seaforth", where I had the privilege to serve for the next 26 years (1974 – 2000).

Lynne and I on the day of my induction in
New Malden, September 1974

My First Church

I was offered the princely sum of ten pounds per week plus expenses as my stipend! It was explained that, at that point, the average income for the church was £28 per week. They paid me ten pounds which left the balance to pay all the other expenses both for the church itself and our accommodation, a two bedroomed flat built behind the church and connected to it, plus gas, electricity, water and telephone etc.

Early days at New Malden, outside the church door

That ten-pound sum in those days was just sufficient to cover food, but things were rather tight. Lynne continued to teach at Parliament Hill School so each morning I dropped her on my motor bike to Morden tube station for her to travel to Kentish Town, then each afternoon I drove up to the school to collect her and bring her home to the flat we were provided with behind the church.

This did not last too long before Lynne's health suffered and she could not continue, so the doctor laid her off on medication for several weeks till she was feeling better. It was obvious Lynne could not continue like this as we left home at 6am each morning and arrived home at 6pm, and then she would work for several hours marking pupil's books and preparing her lessons.

Thus, she tendered her resignation at the school to finish at Christmas, but still needed to work out her notice. Elizabeth's parents (Lynne's RE pupil) kindly offered accommodation in their home during the week, a five-minute walk from the school, so I drove Lynne up on my motorcycle on Monday mornings and collected her on Friday evenings until the end of term.

From this point on Lynne became a housewife

and subsequently a mother too, as our son Martyn was born in 1975 and Clair our daughter in 1979. Lynne did not return to teaching till both children had started school themselves.

With permission of the church, I sought part-time work at "Boots the Chemist" in Kingston Market Place, where I worked each afternoon Monday to Friday, doing my church work in the mornings and evenings. This helped somewhat with my income and the church raised my stipend to £15 per week.

However, with a growing family, finances were still tight so I sought a job using my previous laboratory qualifications. At this point I was preaching twice a week on Sundays and preparing a Bible Study midweek too, as well as other pastoral ministry and leadership meetings. I found a post as a laboratory technician at a grammar school in Wimbledon where they wanted me to totally revamp their laboratories. I was given a contract where a month's notice was required to resign the post. I well remember pacing around our lounge wondering whether or not I should sign the contract.

I was in somewhat of a turmoil because I felt I should be full-time in the church, not in a secular job. However, I prayed, took a deep breath, signed the contract and then ran to the post box to send it off before I changed my mind.

Once I had done that, a real peace came over me as I had an assurance that it was all in God's hands. That night, Lynne woke me up in the middle of the night to tell me the Lord had woken her and given her a message. He had said that he wanted me full-time in the church, not in a secular job, and she was to apologise to me for putting pressure on me to bring in more finance. Wow! My response was, "Why on earth didn't you tell me before I signed the contract?"

In the circumstances we decided I would complete the task I had been asked to achieve at the school starting in the January, resigning at the end of the summer term. It proved a hard task to complete, trying to maintain the ministry at church and the extra job, but with the Lord's help I achieved it, and we went away on holiday in August knowing I would be able to take up the full-time reins in the church on our return.

When we came back from holiday, a letter was awaiting us from the church secretary informing us that the church had met while we were away and decided that, because we had stepped out in faith, they would too, so were doubling our stipend to £30 plus expenses. They said that if the income did not improve by Christmas they would go into the red. However, the Lord blessed the giving and not only were they able to provide for us, but in succeeding years were able to support ten of our then 60 members, at 50% of their faith targets as they served the Lord in mission both in the UK and overseas. Jehovah Jireh is indeed a great provider!

When I started ministry at New Malden, we had twenty members, but I stayed long enough as their pastor to see the ups and downs of church life with the congregation growing at one stage to 120, though we were down to 50 when I eventually moved on to Staplehurst in 2000.

In the initial stages of my ministry, I felt I was part of an evangelical church in name, which to my mind was not being evangelical. So I embarked on a teaching series of practical evangelism, especially noting all I had learnt with Campus Crusade. At the conclusion of the series, I felt the Lord ask me what I thought I had achieved, to which my response was, not very much. I felt a bit like the disciples must have felt as recorded in

Luke chapter 5 when challenged by the Lord to put out into the deeper water. Peter answered, "Master, we've worked hard all night and haven't caught anything". The Lord's response to me was to tell me to, "Sow seeds for mission and leave the growth to me. I will add to this church!"

Thus, I began with Genesis chapter twelve on Abraham's call and over time began to sow into people's hearts the desire to become a sending church. The first to respond was a young man completing university, who felt called to serve with "Operation Mobilisation" and others followed, until as previously mentioned, ten of our congregation moved out into mission both here in the UK and overseas.

During that time, God was faithful to His promise and had begun adding people to our congregation with people coming to faith in Christ, or Christians moving into the area and being led to our church. Our church was not far from Motspur Park Station, on the line from London Waterloo through Raynes Park and out to Effingham Junction, and we paid for an advert on the station pointing people to our church. Several people came as a result!

The Lord's Provision

While at New Malden there were many testimonies and illustrations of God's provision for us as a family, and stories of His abundant grace in the lives of the congregation and some of those follow in this next section. They proved to us just how caring our heavenly Father is!

Having already mentioned our holidays, I start with the Lord's wonderful provision for us as a family. We were introduced to a Christian couple, Dick and Paula, who owned a dairy farm at Summercourt in Cornwall, and offered full-board and accommodation for those serving in Christian ministry. They asked for no money saying, "Give what you can afford and if that is nothing, that's fine, for the Lord makes it up to us. Over the year it all balances out and we are never out of pocket".

We were able as a family to use this facility for around 15 years and we have amazing memories of wonderful times together. The Lord always provided us with some finances to be able to give, to help cover our expenses and we established a wonderful bond with that couple, again with whom, we are still in touch. As we were preparing for our first visit to Cornwall, Lynne said, "We can't go without any money to offer, we have no money in the bank, perhaps we should cancel". I responded indicating that the Lord God, our heavenly Father wanted us to have a holiday and would therefore provide. Lynne was not so sure.

At 7:30am on the morning I was packing the car to go away, the postman arrived with a letter from a friend containing a cheque for £100. We now had His provision for this journey and finance to bless our friends. "Thank you, Lord." Then just before we left, our youth Bible class leader turned up to pass on a gift for our holiday from the young people. How humbling that was!

Incidentally, we had an orange Suzuki 100cc motorbike for transport which we bought new when we were a couple living in London, and that suited us well for getting about in the city until our first child came along. A couple in the church then came and offered us their Mini-traveller estate car, so this greatly helped us travelling as a family and we in turn felt we should give away our motorbike, passing it to friends who had no transport at all. Over the years, changes of transport were covered by the Lord and we were privileged to have three or four cars given us as the need arose.

I have to say in those early days of ministry when the congregation was small and the finances tight that we had to pray about all our financial needs, but the Lord never let us down and so often miraculously provided just when needed.

We had no television or music centre, just the basic furniture in New Malden, because the flat in Kentish Town had been fully furnished and Lynne had chosen to receive her superannuation back when she left school, which enabled us to buy those basics for the New Malden flat. Others observed our lack and specifically gave gifts which enabled us to buy such luxuries. How good is the Lord!

When Martyn was due to go to secondary school, we had no money to buy the uniform so we prayed together asking for the Lord's provision. Again, a specific gift was given from friends unaware of our need. I can remember a time sitting at our dining room table with the family waiting to eat tea, however we had no food. I said we should say grace and give thanks to the Lord, to which the children piped up asking what the point was. As I finished praying, there was a ring at the door bell. As I opened the front door I was confronted by a bag of groceries. I dashed out to see who had delivered them but no one was in sight. Again, we were very grateful for the Lord's provision.

The need to pray for the Lord to provide was something we tried to build into the lives of our children too. At one point Martyn was desperate to have a BMX bike. We encouraged him to pray about it. A few days later an envelope popped through the letter box addressed to Martyn. An anonymous note inside said the enclosed money was for him to purchase a bike. We hadn't told anyone except the Lord. What a delightful surprise for us all!

Perhaps one of the most encouraging stories was when the church hall, built in the 1950s, had passed its "sell by date" and was falling apart. We knew we needed a new building but only a few thousand pounds were available in our building fund. Together with the treasurer we approached our bank manager to negotiate a loan, which thankfully was agreed upon, so work could begin. The old building was demolished, the site cleared and a new pre-fabricated building craned onto the site. Before we needed to put the loan in place, a plethora of gifts came into church funds enabling us to fully cover the bills, a total around £50,000; the Lord showing us He is indeed Jehovah Jireh, the Great Provider.

The Father Heart Of God

I mentioned earlier that over the years, I discovered a number of people struggled in their understanding of God as their Father. I was so grateful for the relationship I had with my dad which enabled me to have a positive understanding of what it meant to have an appreciation of the Father heart of God. However, even though we had a great relationship, he too had his faults like all of us, and one of them affected me in my ministry. As a church leader, I could share vision with the rest of the leadership team and while they all agreed with what I shared, that was fine and we could go ahead. But if they raised concerns or disagreed with me, instead of holding my ground and developing my suggestion further with them till hopefully, in prayer we could see eye to eye, I would immediately back down. Wrong!

It was a lady in the church with whom we shared this dilemma, who said to me that there must be something in my past relationship with my father which was affecting my willingness to stand firm. As I prayed, I remembered as I was growing up, that whenever my dad and I disagreed over something, he always won the argument, even frustratingly when I **knew** I was right. I always backed down for the sake of peace.

The Lord showed me how that was now affecting my leadership decisions. The next Sunday evening I confessed that need of deliverance to the congregation and asked them to pray for me, and as a result the Lord began helping me to be more confident in sharing with the leadership when I was confident of knowing I had heard the Lord. This was not a "lording it" over people, but a willingness to cast ourselves on the Lord for further clarity when we found some disagreement amongst us. Very healthy!

I was out visiting another congregation one Sunday and was speaking on this very subject of the Father heart of God, when following the teaching, I offered people prayer on this matter. Several came forward but one young lady stood with her head bowed down. I was prompted by the Lord to lift her head with the instruction given to look into my eyes. As she did so, I found words given to me along these lines, "Look into my eyes my child and know I love and value you. You are my special child and I long for a deeper relationship with you". The young lady burst into tears and cried out, "How did you know, how did you know?" My response was, "How did I know what?"

What followed gave an explanation of her situation into which I was able to pray and seek God's healing. Apparently, as she was growing up, she constantly looked into her father's face seeking his loving approval but he would never ever look into her eyes and grant the desire of her heart to see his approving eyes and experience his love. As a result, she had come to believe that God would not approve of her either, but this day He spoke into her life and assured her of His love and the special relationship He had with her. That had a truly healing and empowering impact.

On another occasion, while away on a house party with our church at Pilgrim Hall in Sussex, during a session one of the members came forward to be prayed over for healing. The Lord said to me that further revelation was needed before I could proceed with healing prayer. I shared this with the congregation and someone said that as they were praying, they saw a picture of a man in the distance but it was very hazy and couldn't identify the person. The gentleman being prayed for ventured a response saying this was his father, and felt the Lord saying he needed to forgive him. He then burst into tears and sobbed uncontrollably for quite a while. Apparently, we learned later that his father had left home when he was six years old leaving him, his brother and mother to fend for themselves. He hadn't been seen since and the son was now in his forties. Through his sobbing he asked the Lord to help him forgive his dad and although he had been angry at his father for leaving them, he admitted he loved him and asked the Lord to save him if he was still alive. I was then able to proceed with prayer for physical as well as emotional healing.

As I was sharing this on my return to New Malden with one of our church leaders who had not been present at the house party, he too burst into tears saying his father had also left home when he was six years old. I needed to pray for him as well. Isn't the Lord amazing bringing healing to two people in very similar circumstances!

While on mission in Yorkshire with the Methodist evangelist, Rob Frost (who in the end was my prayer partner for over 20 years) and having preached in the Methodist Church where I was to lead an outreach for a week, I was given hospitality by the church 80-year-old leading steward. Once inside her home she declared she was delighted to have me on her own because she wanted to talk to me privately. She declared, "You know about the Holy Spirit don't you", and then said she had been unable to talk to anyone at the church about the matter. She wanted me to tell her about the ministry of the Holy Spirit. I shared with her for about an hour on the subject and then she asked me to pray with her to be baptised with the Holy Spirit.

As I prepared to do so, the Lord spoke to me and said, "Don't pray for her yet as she has a problem with her father". I mentioned this to her and she immediately exploded in anger. "My father nearly ruined my marriage; he was always interfering and we had to keep a distance". I explained the need to forgive her dad before the Lord would allow me to pray for her to be filled with the Spirit. And in tears she did so straight away, saying how much she loved him and asking metaphorically why he had chosen to do what he did as she had, had such a good relationship with him while she was single. After her confession was blurted out, the Lord released me to pray for her to be baptised in the Holy Spirit and she was greatly blessed. Her heavenly Father seemingly lifted her into his arms and melted her with His love, she described afterwards. After that she joined in mission teams herself for the next five years until failing health precluded such further activity.

My final illustration comes much later in my ministry having moved on from New Malden in 2000 to Staplehurst Free Church in Kent. One of our leaders, Kate Henry, spent five years as a missionary with Latin Link in Ecuador and I was invited to speak at their field, annual conference. In one of the sessions, I spoke about the "Father Heart of God" and having done so, a local pastor from Santo Domingo who was also at the conference with his wife and children, came to me after the session to talk about his difficult relationship with his father and how that had affected his ministry. I was privileged to pray with him then, but that prompted him to invite me back another year to minister to his congregation on that very subject, the "Father Heart of God", resulting in much further blessing. I was even privileged to lead one of the non-Christian fathers, who attended that weekend to the Lord! It is good, many years later, still to be in touch with this church on social media and by email.

I am in the centre of the picture overleaf, sat next to Xavier and his wife, Lizette. I was later to visit his church in Santo Domingo, and to have the privilege of speaking at two church houesparties he had arranged, one for the ladies of his church and the other for the men. We still keep in touch.

Clive with the Latin Link missionary team (Xavier and Lizette to my right) - when I visited their annual conference I spoke on the Father heart of God

Xavier and Lizette - Pastors at Santo Domingo, Ecuador, 2011

The Lord helped me to further understand His heart for loving His people as I studied further in the Gospel of John. I believe that Jesus was the most secure person the world has ever known, which enabled Him to function effectively in obedience to His Father. In John 5:19-20 Jesus says, "I tell you the truth, the Son can do nothing by himself; he can only do what he sees the Father doing, because whatever the Father does, the Son also does. For the Father loves the Son and shows him all he does."

At His baptism, the Father spoke to Jesus saying, "This is my beloved Son in whom I am well pleased". So, right at the beginning of His earthly ministry Jesus is assured that He is loved by God the Father. I believe it is this assurance of being loved that gives Jesus the ability to do what God asks of him. I must confess when I read this passage in Mark's gospel chapter one, while I was in hospital as described in my preface, I thought to myself, "This is not fair Lord. Jesus has not yet started his ministry and you are already telling him that you are pleased with him". "That's your problem", was His reply. "You think you have to do something for me, to gain my approval. That is not true. You are loved and approved of, precisely because you are my child and not because of what you do for me". What a release and revelation that was to my spirit! It was because He was loved by His Father that Jesus was secure enough to do whatever was asked of him by God. The Lord wants us to have that same assurance of love and security so we will be enabled to function in obedience to Him.

If you do a study in the prayers of Jesus, you will notice how He addresses His prayers to God as His father, and when the disciples observe Him praying as recorded in Luke chapter eleven, they ask Him to teach them to pray. He replies, "When you pray, say, Our Father who art in heaven, hallowed be your name". He is suggesting the greatest priority we have in prayer is to know and experience a relationship with God as our Father and to worship Him. In John 14:30-31 Jesus says, "I will not speak with you much longer, for the prince of this world is coming. He has no hold on me, but the world must learn that I love the Father and that I do exactly what my Father has commanded me". How do people know we love the Father? Not because we say so, but because they too, see that we do exactly what He asks of us. Wow!

Are we secure enough in His love to be able to do exactly what the Lord asks of us? In John 16:32 Jesus says, speaking to His disciples before He is arrested "A time is coming, and has come when you will be scattered, each to his own home. You will leave me all alone. Yet I am not alone, for my Father is with me". His assurance of God's love, enabled Him to go to the cross assured that the Lord His Father was with him.

Realising this truth adds even more depth of understanding to the terrible loss Jesus feels on the cross when He is seemingly surprised at the enormity of the weight of the world's sin upon Him and cries out, "My God, my God, why have you forsaken me?" It is because we need to know we are loved by God in order to function well as Christians, that in my opinion, the majority of people have a problem in one way or another in this area and need prayer to be assured, they are loved by God.

Over the years I have been in ministry, it seems to me it is vitally important to stress the "Father heart of God", and I did make a promise many years ago to the Lord that I would speak on the subject the first time I had an opportunity to preach in a new church to me. I have endeavoured to keep that promise and nearly always find people coming forward for prayer precisely because their understanding of God as their Father, in one way or another is affected by their past or present relationship with their earthly fathers. Now I must stress here, that I too have made my mistakes in the bringing up of my children, and have needed to apologise to them on occasions, stressing that God is far greater than any problems I may have caused, and He would bring healing to them, should they need it.

The Wider Local Church

One of the joys of ministry in New Malden for a long period was working with other churches in a variety of ways. I mentioned before, Garth Moody, the pastor at Wimbledon Congregational Church. He is the tallest gentleman in glasses in the centre of the picture below which records an early Easter morning meeting for all churches on the highest point of Wimbledon Common.

I am holding a song sheet in my hand as we declare the praises of God together. Norman Moss, the minister of Wimbledon Baptist church, whose vision it was to hold such services, joined with us, his head capped, with his back to the photographer. These services took place over many years and we also collaborated together in holding a "Mustard Seed" children's mission each summer for many years, also on Wimbledon Common near the windmill. These mission teams were sponsored by Scripture Union, and while the majority of team members came from local churches, some came from various parts of the country. I was delighted to serve on these teams, and thrilled to see a good number of young people give their lives to Jesus.

"Mustard Seed Team" outside Wimbledon Baptist Church

Garth Moody, Norman Moss and I started a weekly meeting for pastors which met for many years, and was a vital ministry for me in order to share my faith with other brothers in other local churches, where we sensed a great measure of accountability and mutual friendship.

Norman and Margaret Moss 2015

We normally met on Tuesday mornings for a couple of hours for prayer and sharing together, a real growth point for my own spiritual maturity as we shared from the

Scriptures and prayed for one another and the surrounding area.

Garth Moody 2013

Our numbers were usually about six to ten depending on availability and holidays etc, however for me, it was a real priority in my diary. In the early 1990's a new move of the Spirit began to touch many nations of the world and one of our colleagues, Malcolm, travelled to Canada to visit one of the centres where there was a great move of the Spirit.

On his return he shared with us all that he had seen and heard, and out of his experience we began to pray for each other. The Lord began to stir in our hearts too and most of us began experiencing such a move of the Spirit in our lives that we couldn't stand in His presence, finding ourselves falling to the floor where the Lord ministered into our lives.

This was both thrilling and challenging as the Lord touched on areas where we needed change, healing and encouragement. This move of the Holy Spirit became known as the "Toronto Blessing" and caused many to be blessed across our nation, although there was some consternation and criticism of the movement too. From my perspective however, I saw many good changes in my own life and the lives of others from my church whom I had known for many years.

People whom I had counselled, who spent time on the floor under the conviction of the Holy Spirit, had been changed radically for the good. "By their fruits they shall be known". Indeed, much good fruit came out of this move of the Holy Spirit. One amazing experience was seeing our regular leaders meeting on a Tuesday morning grow to several hundred people attending each week for prayer and healing which continued for a considerable number of months.

Our working together in the area brought fruit in other ways too. We held a number of outreach and teaching meetings for years in local churches, even hiring the Wimbledon town hall and Wimbledon Theatre (for a Luis Palau Crusade). The Baptist church played host to Prayer and Bible Weeks where I "cut my teeth" on speaking at larger meetings, as well as Prayer Days, hosted by Intercessors for Britain. In New Malden we held many Prayer days and conferences run by the Lydia Ladies Prayer movement and quite often I ran a crèche for such events in order to release our own church ladies to be able to attend.

At one point we as a group of ministers felt the Lord leading us to appoint a schools' worker sponsored by The London City Mission (LCM) and we started a "Prayer for Education" group, which ran for many years, and was still running when I moved out of the area in 2000. I was asked to chair this group which met on a monthly basis praying for school children and staff in the London Borough of Merton.

Peter Kendrick, from LCM, was appointed as the schools' worker, in which he served for some twenty years, only stopping when he retired sometime in the past five years. We were fortunate enough to establish, with the support of the LCM, a local schools' Christian resource centre which, with books, teaching materials, films and DVDs, for loan, served many schools and their teachers, in aiding the teaching of the R.E. national curriculum in the local area.

Peter Kendrick on a visit to Israel in 2014

Christian Friends Of Israel

It was while I was at New Malden that I began to discover an interest in Israel, and the place it had in the purposes of God. Two of my fellow leaders grew in their understanding of this subject and both were later to become Directors of a Christian Ministry called "Christian Friends of Israel". Derek White initially founded the UK branch of the "International Christian Embassy, Jerusalem", which later changed its name to "Christian Friends of Israel". I was invited to become a trustee of both.

Emblem of Christian Friends of Israel

Derek continued in this role until he retired, when another of my ex-leaders at New Malden, Roy Thurley, became the director of CFI, serving for a number of years. My initial interest in praying for Israel came at a point when the Lord spoke into my life with the invitation, "Will you pray for My people as a dying man cries out for his mother?"

Myself, together with Roy Thurley and Jenny Forbes, fellow CFI Trustees, visiting with a member of CFI Jerusalem

I agreed to commit myself to such a request without fully understanding at the time what the Lord's request fully meant. It was only many years later when on a visit to Israel, I heard our guide talk of how her son had been a tank commander in one of the recent wars between Israel and Hezbollah in Lebanon. Apparently, his crew had told her afterwards that as he led them into battle, he had cried out to his mother saying he loved her and hoped he would return. At this point the Lord's original request to me... "as a dying man cries out for his mother", suddenly had its full impact, and I was deeply moved.

I remained a board member of CFI for 35 years until the Lord allowed me to lay down that role. I still pray regularly for the peace of Jerusalem and God's people Israel.

I will add in here another indication of God's loving provision. I longed to visit Israel and take my family, but my income would not really furnish such a trip. One day in my reading, I read Job 22:27-30 and the Lord highlighted verse 28 to me, "You will pray to him, and he will hear you, and you will fulfil your vows. **What you decide on will be done** and light will shine on your ways". Lord, I mused, if I decide to go to Israel with my family, are you saying it will happen? I was reminded of,

"Whatever you ask for in prayer, believe that you have received it and it will be yours" (Mark 11:24). I went to one of my fellow leaders, shared my discovery and prayer regarding a trip to Israel. We decided together that I would go with my family however and whenever, the Lord made it possible. He agreed to keep this confidential.

On the following Sunday, after the service, one of the members of the church, asked for a quiet word. He explained that for some time he had been praying about me going to Israel, and that just that week the Lord had released him to go ahead with his plans. He had contacted Derek White, discovered he was leading a group to Israel, and booked a place on that trip for Lynne, myself, Martyn and Clair. I gasped that I could not afford it, but was told not to worry because he was paying! What an amazing answer to prayer! We had a fantastic trip and we all loved the experience. Thank you, Lord!

Moving back to the passage in Job 22, after further study, I preached a message much later on verses 29-30 which I felt the Lord was leading me to, in order to encourage intercessors. "When men are brought low and you say, "Lift them up!" then he will save the downcast. He will deliver even one who is

Derek White, at his 90th birthday celebration, February 2018

not innocent, who will be delivered through the cleanness of your hands." My encouragement was to not give up on those for whom we pray, who seem to actually get worse rather than better in terms of their relationship with God, and to keep pressing on in prayer even though they may not be innocent. As I was preaching a lady stood up in my congregation rather excitedly saying, "That works, I know it does because it has worked in my family!"

She went on to explain that her father-in-law had been a godless man, blaspheming, gambling and drinking. She had been praying for him for years. Then he contracted throat cancer, had his voice box removed and could no longer speak. One day he wrote a message, while still in hospital, to his nurse asking to see the hospital chaplain. The chaplain came and talked to her father-in-law about Jesus, saying that if he wanted to receive Christ he should pray quietly, phrase by phrase the Lord's Prayer as the Chaplain prayed it too.

What amazed everyone there at the time, chaplain and nurses alike, was that this man, who had no voice box, prayed the Lord's Prayer **out loud** right the way through, then with a smile on his face laid back on the pillow and died, entering into the presence of the Lord! What a thrilling testimony to underline the message I was in the middle of preaching!

Moving On

After 20 years as the pastor in New Malden I felt it was time to move on. I had given all I knew how to the church, but needed to cast myself upon the Lord for His direction for the future.

Being involved with an independent evangelical church, and not part of a denomination, I had no one to turn to, in a hierarchy above me, for advice about moving to another church. Baptists have their moderators, Anglicans have their bishops, but we had no one in that sort of capacity.

I was directed to an organisation which was part of the Evangelical Alliance, with whom we as a church were associated, called "Dovetail". They took ministers' CVs and churches' pro-formas and endeavoured to pass on CVs to churches requesting help with seeking new pastors. Several churches requested me to go to preach, but nothing ever came of it.

I did at one point receive a possible invitation to follow up as a result of going on mission with my prayer partner of 26 years, Rob Frost, to Nelson in Lancashire.

So how did I meet Rob and become such good friends? It began at a time when Rob was the minister of Mitcham Methodist Church in Surrey, about six miles away from me in New Malden.

Rob Frost, my prayer partner for over 20 years

Rob wrote, each week, a "Dear Rob" column, in a local newspaper called the "Guardian". One week I was phoned by the paper to ask my comments on a new film out at the time called "The Life of Brian", a seeming parody on the life of Jesus. I said I couldn't really answer their question as I had never seen it, but understood it made a mockery of the life of Christ. That same week Rob was given a ticket by the newspaper asking him to review the film and the next edition of the paper had a front-page headline, "Ministers argue about the Life of Brian".

Having written his review, the paper took parts of his wording out of context and made it seem as though we were arguing, although we had never met. He phoned me up apologising profusely saying he agreed with my perspective and had complained to the paper for what they had done.

They gave him some money and asked him to take me out to lunch by way of their apology for any offence caused. We met, had lunch, enjoyed fellowship, and prayed together. What an amazing turn around that was. It brought to mind Joseph's words to his brothers that the circumstances were evil but the Lord meant it for good.

So, began a 26-year friendship with Rob, meeting together about every six weeks, until sadly he was untimely taken from us, with cancer, at the age of 54.

Getting back to the visit to Nelson for a mission, I went to preach there several times and it all looked very positive, with the church leadership even offering to help us purchase a house in the town once the church meeting had affirmed my call to serve them as their next pastor. In the event the required number of votes was not obtained and that possible door of opportunity was firmly closed.

I was cast back on the Lord as I felt I had run out of steam to continue my ministry in New Malden. However, the Lord re-invigorated and re-envisioned me and I continued to minister there for another few years.

In the year 2000, the Lord gave me a vision for a year of evangelism in the church. We employed a "Seed Team", a husband-and-wife couple provided by Rob Frost's ministry "Share Jesus International", to work with us for the year, culminating in a week's mission to be held in August 2000. It was while these plans were being formulated in the latter half of 1999, that I was approached by a church in Staplehurst Kent, who had received my CV

Staplehurst Free Church

from "Dovetail" and were interested to meet with me in order to progress the matter further.

I met with the leadership team in December 1999, and then went to preach at the church in February 2000. They still wanted to take things further, so I went with Lynne to stay with them for two days, at their request, where I met with all the house groups and prayer groups, effectively being interviewed by 70 or 80 people!

This left Lynne and I with a dilemma. At the time, she had been teaching at Chessington Community college for some 16 years, and if we were to move, she needed to resign giving a terms notice, and apply for a teaching post in Kent, near to Staplehurst. Being a Wealden village, it only had a primary school, and she was a maths teacher in a secondary school. She applied for a post at Angley school in Cranbrook, the nearest secondary school to Staplehurst, five miles away, went for an interview, and was offered the job before I heard back from the church.

By Easter 2000, the church had held a church meeting and unanimously called me to serve them as pastor. It was just like the Lord, to call me out of New Malden while I was in a busy year of evangelism. I told the Church in Staplehurst I couldn't join them until September, once we had completed our week's mission in New Malden. So it was, that after a very successful week of evangelism, we had our final service at Seaforth Avenue, New Malden after 26 years, and moved down to Kent, to a new ministry in Staplehurst.

Easter People

Another ministry that opened up for Lynne and I, as a result of our friendship with Rob and Jacqui Frost, was an invitation to be a part of a ministry team Rob was putting together, to run a week-long conference/holiday event called Easter People. It was initially for the Methodist church in which Rob, by this time, had been set aside as a full-time evangelist.

I well remember Rob asking me in one of our meetings what I thought of his new plans and the vision to take over a holiday camp at Camber Sands for a Christian event around Easter time. I was bowled over by the enormity of his vision, but eventually he was able to gound it, and that first event actually took place with Donald English, the president of the Methodist Church being the key-note speaker.

He spoke each day from the book of Ephesians and I found myself quite often in tears of joy and appreciation thinking to myself, "God, I did not know you are as amazing as this!" The conference was a resounding success with about 1200 people in attendance, but when Rob visited the nearby town of Rye, he soon realised that the town was totally untouched by this Christian event, so he re-vamped his vision for the future.

His heart was to touch the local community by Easter People coming to the area. For the next 18 years, Easter People went to various towns around the country, including Bournemouth, Torquay, Scarborough, Blackpool and Llandudno.

We used various venues in each town including churches, theatres and public parks with evangelistic teams bringing the good news of Jesus, as well as the opportunity to encourage and build-up believers. This event grew from the initial 1200 to several thousand people from across the Christian community, not just the Methodist Church.

For me, it meant the amazing opportunity to learn to minister God's word to far larger audiences than I had heretofore experienced. Our involvement as a couple spanned a twenty-year period across both churches I was privileged to serve.

Visits To Overseas Mission Fields

I mentioned earlier that at one stage in New Malden, ten of our 60 members were involved in mission overseas or in the UK. Having quite so many was a real stretch on the available funds to support them, as well as the church and ministry at home. However, we resolved that we should endeavour to support them to the best of our ability, and decided we should offer them 50% of their faith target. This meant that if say, their faith target was £400 per month, we as a church would send them £200 per month. The Lord amazingly provided in order that we were all kept afloat!

I was personally challenged about visiting these missionaries at least once in each period of time they were out on the field, because as members of the church, just like members at home, they needed pastoral visitation and encouragement. Having read the autobiography of a missionary to China amongst the Lisu people, J. O. Fraser, I noted he always kept in touch regularly with his home church and supporters. His theory was that "his best work on the field was done by his intercessors back home", so believed it vital to keep them regularly updated.

I therefore exhorted our missionaries to write at least once a month to the church back home. I also felt it very important that the church was involved in their call to whichever country and mission agency that trained and sent them, so I found myself visiting mission agency headquarters when our members were being interviewed and trained. These were our members, and I sensed it right not to just hand them over to the agency, but to be a part of the journey of checking out their call to mission alongside them. In the end I was privileged to travel to, and speak at, churches and field team conferences in Sudan, Chad, Sri Lanka, the Philippines, France, Germany, Eire, while at New Malden, and Ecuador while in Staplehurst.

At latitude 0000 on a visit to Ecuador

This privilege not only gave me opportunities to visit and see what our missionaries were doing on the field, but to pray with them about their joys, sorrows and plans for the future. On my return to the UK, I was more able to effectively communicate (in addition to their letters) the extent of the various ministries to the sending church, our congregation.

Cotopaxi Volcano, Quito, Ecuador from my bedroom window

These were very special times for me as I learnt so much and felt the Lord enlarge my vison to encourage the churches I served, to embrace overseas mission, and to continue to seek to be sending churches.

The Move To Staplehurst Free Church

My first priority on arriving in Staplehurst was to enlist the church in helping me to deliver a letter to the whole village community, which at that time numbered about 5000 people. I wrote telling them of my arrival and welcoming them to visit the church at any stage. That at least let people know of what was happening at the Free Church and enabled easy openings in conversation. At least two people responded, one attending the church as a result and is still with us 24 years later, while the other asked for help and prayer. I am still in touch with them today, although they attend a local Church of England congregation. It also bore fruit with an invitation to take part in the local primary school assemblies which I continued on a regular basis right up to my retirement in 2013.

It would be good to add in here how the Lord taught me a lesson about guidance in hearing His call to Staplehurst. Having heard very clearly Him speaking to me back in 1974 that "You are my man for New Malden", I was expecting Him to grant me a similar call to Staplehurst. Perhaps, "I release you from New Malden and am sending you to

Staplehurst", or something along those lines, but I waited in total silence in that regard. The fact that leaders at New Malden told me they sensed regretfully, that it was time for me to move on, that Lynne had been offered a job locally, and that the church meeting had sent me a unanimous call, did not move me.

It was not until I read the story of David in 2 Samuel 5:18-25 where he had to enquire of the Lord on two separate occasions what to do when fighting the Philistines and received two different answers, that I realised I was nearly missing God's call to me to respond positively to the church's call in Staplehurst to join them as their pastor. He was showing me quite clearly what He wanted me to do but because I was prescribing what I wanted Him to do in order for me to respond, I almost missed His word. Thankfully, I listened and responded positively, accepting the call to join them! How important it is to cultivate a listening ear to the Lord's voice!

Housing

Having to move from New Malden, where the church had provided initially a two bedroomed flat and later, a four bedroomed tied house, to Staplehurst, the church here did not have any manse, so we needed to find accommodation in order to live here. The church said they would pay for rented property for us if we could find such a house available. Fortunately, a friend of ours, Kim Cook, who was at the time an estate agent in Cranbrook, had one such property available in Staplehurst, a small three bedroomed house in Tomlin Close for rent at £600 per month. We gladly took this, moving into the house during July 2000 before we finally left New Malden. We were rather cramped but managed storing excess stuff in a shed and the garage.

Our accountant advised us to ask the church to pay the rent for us, lowering our stipend accordingly, in order to have a favourable position with the inland revenue! The church said, that, should we change our mind at any time in order to purchase a house in the village, they would give us that rent to help pay any mortgage. Interestingly a few years previously a couple in our church in New

Malden advised us to enter the mortgage ladder and begin to purchase something for ourselves. We managed to buy a flat in Worthing on mortgage, for the amazing sum of £32,500 which we used for a number of years as a holiday home. We did try to sell this flat before coming to Staplehurst in order to release finance for us to purchase something here but to no avail.

After a year in our rental, we put the flat on the market again and sold it within three weeks for £90,000. This enabled us to purchase the bungalow we are now living in, in Iden Crescent, using the sale price as a deposit for the bungalow which we purchased for £150,000. The sale price of our flat provided the deposit and the balance we took as a mortgage, which amazingly we were able to pay off within a shorter period of time than originally envisaged.

About Staplehurst Free Church

This church was founded in 1968 by three families who moved into the village not previously knowing one another, but finding no evangelical witness in their perception, and amazingly meeting one another, started a house church in their own homes. The founding families were Stan and Doff Twort, John and Irene Dolding, together with Robert and Marion Taylor. Church services and Bible studies were held in one home, while Sunday school was held in another. As the church grew, an extension was added to act as a meeting room at the rear of the Taylor's home in Thatcher Road. The church continued to grow and they hired a variety of buildings in the village to hold services, including the scout hut.

Robert Taylor decided to move from Thatcher Road to larger premises, "Tall Trees", in Station Road which had previously belonged to a toy maker who had converted an old stable block in the grounds to a factory and shop to make and sell his toys. This old stable was in turn transformed into useable premises for the church to hold services, Sunday school, and midweek bible studies and youth meetings. It included a baptistery for the baptism of adult believers to follow the Lord Jesus through the waters of baptism.

Some 35 years ago the church was remarkably able to purchase the village hall which was up for sale.

The front building of Staplehurst Free Church - note the rounded roof of the old aircraft hangar to the right rear of the photo

This, in turn, had been built in 1925 using the framework of a 1914/18 World War one aircraft hangar. But perhaps we should go back to the Opening Ceremony of the Staplehurst Village Hall in April 1925 at 5pm, using the report given to the church by village historian, Anita Thompson.

It was described, at the time, as the fine New Village Hall, erected "at an inclusive cost of nearly £1200, of which about £500 has been raised." It was 60 x 30 feet, 20 feet high, a wooden building on brick foundations "and quite a model for other villages of a similar type," with up-to-date heating and a stage from the Arts League. This stage was most unusual because it was raked, higher at the back than at the front, just like a professional theatre. The hall had an excellent colour scheme, said the "Kent Messenger", a local newspaper. It was connected with an annexe by a covered in way, having connected the main hall to an old Methodist Mission Hall which having served a useful purpose in the village for some years, had now become integrated into the new building. A wish-list of future hopes was read out: "there will be a reading room and a club for men and women, and there will be various games, films and amusements, including billiards etc."

The corridor connecting the annex to the main church building

The committee was to be representative of the whole village and the village club was re-starting. In the evening, after the tea, there was a highly successful concert which mingled popular London actors with home-grown performers (such as Mr T.W. Cole, accompanist, and Mr Stanley Ladd, who sang a solo). And on Thursday 24th April 1925 there was a grand opening dance with the music supplied by the Palais Dance Orchestra, from Maidstone.

Colonel Cornwallis, who performed the opening ceremony, praised the hall as "one of the first examples of village community effort", and independent of government help, most praiseworthy. The annexe had come with the site, but the new building behind it was two-thirds of an aeroplane hangar from the first world war, a little rotten around the bottom edges, which had therefore been trimmed and heightened by the brick wall foundations. Its height indoors made it perfect for badminton, as the bowstring roof trusses were tucked well up. Later on, a ceiling was added, which made badminton play more like table tennis!

In February 1988, at a meeting in the old School (opened in 1873) it was decided to buy those school buildings for the parish, and to sell the Village Hall, which needed urgent restoration. The roof of the former aircraft hangar was crumbling, so were the foundation walls and the various joints between the disparate buildings which made up the total area. It was, however, seen as a very useful site by the UK Evangelisation Trust to which the Free Church members had become affiliated, especially as they were now outgrowing the facilities afforded them in the old stable block at "Tall Trees".

In 1989 the members bought the Village Hall in spite of the fact that it had a limited life expectancy. Yet with care and application, it lasted a further 20 years, which isn't bad going. The congregation were very caring in their ongoing maintenance.

The main worship hall during a wedding service

Robert and Marion Taylor felt "called" to move on to a new area, and a part-time pastor was appointed, Tony Willis, who served for five years before he retired. The church had now grown to around 60 or 70 people with a number of children, and as a result the church stepped out in faith in 2000 to "call" their first full-time pastor. This is where I appeared on the scene, arriving with 26 years ministry experience in New Malden evangelical church in Surrey. During the following years the church continued to grow until numbers topped over one hundred, with all the families and children who were involved.

By 2005 the church building, despite our loving care and attention, had become dangerous. We took the decision to demolish and rebuild. We did not have a very large building fund, indeed it only amounted to £11,000, but we stepped out in faith and prayed for God's provision, implementing a number of fund-raising activities while also applying for grants.

We put together a team of people who helped us through this building phase, which included members who were builders, a project manager, a company director, and a solicitor. Working together they took a great weight of responsibility, and steered us carefully through all the necessary arrangements to form a company and to arrange for the new building to eventually be built and opened. A brand-new resource for the community.

The "Final Fling" inside Staplehurst Free Church before demolition

During this period, which in the end amounted to five years, we were most grateful to be able to use the local primary school for our morning services and special events, the village hall for our toddler's club and youth activities, and the United Reformed Church building for our evening services and any midweek activities.

Demolition of the old building 2005

Ground-breaking ceremony with Helen Grant MP, Eric Hotson Mayor, Richard Lusty, Borough Councillor and Clive Jones Pastor in March 2011

The new building in progress

We were thrilled to open the new building in time for Christmas 2012 at the cost of one million two hundred thousand pounds, just four months before I retired in April 2013.

While we have a mortgage to pay for the final amount still outstanding, we are grateful to the Lord that finance was always available to pay the various bills as they arose. While we did have some gifts from various churches, individuals and grant making bodies, the majority of the monies came from church members, who gave sacrificially. I must confess there were times when I thought, "Help Lord, what have I committed this church to", when I saw the enormity of the funds required, but my past experiences in seeing my heavenly Father provide, enabled me to encourage the church to keep on track. Over the years, with interest free loans and successive gifts from anonymous givers, we are nearing the completion of outstanding mortgage payments.

Clive Jones & Ryan Ahern, SFC pastors 2000-2017

The new pastor Ryan Ahern, who took over from me, had been a member of the church with his wife Val, for many years, and I had had the privilege of mentoring him in the leadership role. We held the official opening of the new building one weekend in April 2013, and I retired the following weekend. Ryan was inducted the following week after my retirement, having served as assistant pastor and a deacon for a number of years.

This was a significant period in the life of the free church. Ryan steered the church through its early days with a new building which we had built with a desire to be a real service and blessing to the community. He himself however, was called to serve another church as pastor, in Surrey in March 2017.

The new church building opened in April 2013

It was very humbling for me to see the completion of this building project just as I retired. "Thank you, Lord, for your great provision!"

The Martyr's Memorial

Soon after I arrived in Staplehurst I was interested to look at what I surmised was the village war memorial located on the crossroads in the centre of the village.

Opening ceremony for the Martyrs Memorial, 1905

I was shocked to find it was a memorial to village residents burnt at the stake in Maidstone, in 1557, during the Marian persecution. I wrote to my church history lecturer from my college days, Dr. Geoffrey Nuttall, mentioning this, and he responded saying that Staplehurst had been a lively centre for protestant reformation back in the 16th and 17th centuries.

I researched further and found that the trial of one of the Martyrs, Edmund Allen, who with his wife, had lived and operated the watermill in Frittenden had been recorded in the Foxe's Book of Martyrs, where he gave a lively and thrilling account of his faith in Christ. He and his wife had been reported to the local vicar at Staplehurst for non-attendance at the Eucharist, and as a result threatened with legal action. They had both escaped to Calais in France but when safely ensconced there, had been challenged by the Lord, "What are you doing here? I want you to witness for me in Kent".

The Allen's duly returned to Frittenden Mill, but on arrival were once again reported to the local vicar, who promptly had them arrested. Following the trial, they were duly executed by burning along with three other ladies from Staplehurst.

As I pondered further the commitment to Christ that these dear people exemplified, the Lord spoke into my heart that He was still working in Staplehurst today fulfilling the prayers of these martyred "saints" of old.

The Martyrs memorial today

What a challenge and encouragement that was to my own devotional life. Here I was, learning afresh that prayers prayed on behalf of others in our families, communities and nations, may not see their fulfilment in our lifetimes, but the Lord never forgets! He always answers the heart cry of His people, but in His own Fatherly way and time!

The Memorial carries this inscription: -

*THE NOBLE ARMY OF MARTYRS
PRAISE THEE.*

*This monument is dedicated
to the Memory of
ALICE POTKINS, JOAN BRADBRIDGE,
and ALICE BENDEN of Staplehurst,
also, of EDMUND ALLEN and his WIFE,
who for the faith suffered death, 1556-1557,
during the Marian Persecution.*

*"We shall by God's grace light such a
Candle in England as shall never be put out."*

*Erected 1904 by Protestants of Staplehurst
and District.*

"Thy Word is Truth"

I have stood several times in front of the memorial, and offered prayers mingled with praise and thanks for the willingness of these faithful saints to make a stand for Jesus that cost them everything. "Lord, give me a similar confidence in you to proclaim fearlessly the wonder of your Gospel."

Some years ago, I discovered someone had smothered the memorial in unwound cassette tape, which I knew was a device used by those involved in black magic back then, to put curses on the objects they covered and surrounded. I was really incensed with a holy indignation and cleared the tape away, praying for the Lord's cleansing. I took the tape and cassette home and tried to burn it but with great difficulty. I did after a while manage it, by using lighter fuel. I asked the Lord for His covering protection around the memorial itself and all the churches and their members in Staplehurst. Thank the Lord for His deliverance!

Lynne's Teaching

Lynne's teaching career began as a maths and RE teacher in 1969, at Parliament Hill Girl's school, in Highgate on the edge of Hampstead Heath, while I worked at Westfield College, Hampstead for the first year of married life, followed by four years at New College, Hampstead, London. She had a break from teaching for several years while the children were young and only started back in the teaching profession once the children, Martyn and Clair, were both in full-time education themselves.

There was a knock at our front door one day, from the head of the maths department at Fleetwood School in Chessington. Dave Reddington, whom we had not met before, asked Lynne if she would be prepared to return to teaching one day a week. Apparently, he had been offered a one-day per week training course, for a year, and he needed to provide a maths teacher to replace him for that period. Taking this as a sign and provision from the Lord, Lynne accepted, as it was fairly easy for her to access the school by train from the railway station in our road, which culminated at Chessington station, right next door to the school. However, being a different area from

Highgate, the mixed sex school was somewhat challenging and necessitated Lynne praying fervently each day as she travelled back to the classroom to ask for the Lord's help!

Lynne remained at this school for 16 years before we moved on to Staplehurst in Kent in 2000, increasing her teaching hours slowly up to three days per week. In this environment she was able, with Dave, who happened to be a Christian too, to set up Christian Unions for both staff and pupils. They saw the Lord move in exciting and unexpected ways, with opportunities to pray with the Head of the school and his deputy. Several staff became Christians. During her time here the name of the school was changed to Chessington Community College. Lynne loved this period of her teaching career and was thrilled to see how the Lord touched the lives of a variety of people. I know she was sad to leave.

From 2000 to 2007 Lynne transferred to Angley School in Cranbrook, again teaching maths. She was also able to establish a small Christian Union for staff who wished to come along. As she neared retirement age, she was offered voluntary redundancy which released some finance to put toward our mortgage aforementioned. This happened in the July of 2007 and she officially retired in

November of that year, which again released another lump sum, which together with a gift from her father, enabled us to pay off our mortgage within six years of starting, instead of the anticipated ten years. We were most grateful to the Lord for this timely provision for our accommodation.

Having left school for a while, Lynne was invited back by her head of maths to do some private tuition on a one-to-one basis with pupils wishing to improve their GCSE grades in maths. She loved the opportunity to teach pupils who actually wanted to learn, continuing for several terms until the funding from the Government for this project ran out. So ended a very exciting and fulfilling teaching career for Lynne.

Succession Planning

Having been in ministry for a number of years, it occurred to me that I needed to pray, think about and plan for the church of which I was leader, to have a replacement pastor if and when the Lord called me to move on. So many churches are faced with the dilemma of how to replace their leader once they receive a resignation from their present one. It seemed to me, as a young leader, that it might be more useful and ideal, if some thought and forward planning was given to such an event before it happened.

In New Malden the Lord began to show me how vital it is to mentor others in leadership so that there could be a smooth transition and handover period as one leader moved on, and another took up the baton, such that the continuing congregation were not left in the lurch. Perhaps, in my particular case, this was important because being an independent evangelical church there was no structure in place, outside of the church, to which we could turn, to seek advice and help when the leader moved on. For instance, in the Anglican church, it is possible and necessary to approach the bishop and his team for direction in this matter. In the Baptist and

URC tradition there is access to area moderators for similar help. But independent free churches had no such structure, hence the need to ask the Lord for His help in such a situation which can occur at any time between perhaps every three to ten years or so.

In my case of course, I didn't move from New Malden until I had been there for 26 years. I asked the Lord for His wisdom and I seemed to hear Him say that I should pray for Him to raise up such future leadership from within the existing congregation. I began to pray over a number of years for Him to do that in my situation. I set myself the task of sharing myself, my gifts and ministry with other leaders, and at one point began to take others with me when I was ministering elsewhere, in order for them to help me and observe how I functioned in different environments.

The apostle Paul tells us in his letters that God gives gifts to each believer in the church so that as we share together those gifts and talents, we can build one another up in our walk in Christ. I saw the biblical idea, from my perspective anyway, was that the Lord would raise up and anoint leaders from within the congregation, to take on positions of pastoral leadership. I was at a leaders' conference at where one of our speakers had just returned from a visit to China, where he told us the average age of leaders within the underground church there was 19 years old. They knew they were likely to be arrested and imprisoned quickly, by the communist authorities, once they took that responsibility seriously. Therefore, they functioned effectively very quickly in order to get the gospel message out as soon as possible, encouraging at the same time, leadership training amongst their peers, so that, should they be arrested, there was always someone else ready to take their place. What an example!

I prayed the Lord would raise up people with a similar heart in our congregation in New Malden. When the time came for me to move on there were two such men in our congregation. Bob had been in the church since he was nine years old, and we had met as young married couples back in 1974 when I first came to the church. He had met his wife Ann when they were both serving as young missionaries with "Operation Mobilisation", before I arrived. He followed me about the whole time I was a pastor there and learnt things from me on the job, so to speak.

Colin, I had met when he was 13, a young man in the church youth group. He followed the Lord Jesus into mission when he left university, serving for a while with "Operation Mobilisation", in Egypt and Sudan, where he married Jean. He trained further, serving the Lord with "WEC International" in Chad, where the Lord used him to translate the New Testament into Chad Arabic. He arrived back into the church in New Malden just before I left, and was able to take up the baton of pastoral leadership from me. In turn, when he moved to another ministry in the north of England a few years later, Bob was called by the church to take his place!

I had been in Staplehurst only about a month, when I saw a new couple appear in our church one Sunday morning, and as they walked up the aisle to take a seat the Lord spoke into my heart and said, "This young man is to be the new leader of this church when you move on". I endeavoured, over succeeding years, to get him to preach in our church but he vehemently refused saying this was not his gifting. Then one day I caught Ryan and his wife, Val, working in the church garden. I asked him again to speak and surprisingly he said yes. Afterwards he said he was surprised himself at his reply. After that (he was brilliant at preaching by the way) I took him on several leadership conferences with me and encouraged him to take on the role of a deacon in our church. After a number of years serving on the leadership team the church recognised his leadership qualities, and invited him to work alongside me as assistant Pastor. I discovered Ryan had a real heart to pray for, and support Israel, and he joined me on a trip we took together with "Christian Friends of Israel" to visit Israel in 2008. This was a real confirmation to me that he was the right man to take SFC on into the future.

Ryan at the Sea of Galilee

Two years before I was due to retire, I shared at a leadership away day, the timing I felt in my heart the Lord had given to me to retire (in the event, at the age of 66). I also shared what the Lord had spoken to me about Ryan back in 2000. This was the first time I had shared this with anyone, apart from Lynne. Ryan burst into tears at my suggesting that he should take over from me, and I asked if I had offended him. He replied, "No, I'm not offended, but the Lord spoke to me last week that He wanted me to be the next minister!"

We were all thrilled and spent the next two years preparing the church, and Ryan and Val, for this new transition in ministry. In the event, we officially opened the new church building one weekend in April 2013, I retired the following weekend, and Ryan was inducted as pastor the weekend after that.

The Lord had done what he had planted in my heart many years before, that He would raise up the next minister from within our congregation. This was, and is the best form, of succession planning! "Thank you, Lord!"

Lynne and I were privileged to be able to stay on in the church, no longer in ministry on the leadership team, but as ordinary members of the church, observing the amazing way Ryan grew into the role the Lord had called him to, serving the church as pastor for four years from 2013 to 2017.

Communion at the entrance of the new building under construction - Ryan Ahern on the left and his wife Val to the right. From Ryan, left to right we have elders Don Elliot and Terence Hawgood together with Adrian Perry, the CEO of the building company, tasked with the project and his wife Sue. All of the group were, at the time, members of Staplehurst Free Church.

"Psarms" Puppets

When I arrived at Staplehurst, the church was already involved in fostering and using well, a puppet ministry, which was extremely effective in school's ministry and family services.

Psarms puppets performing in Staplehurst Primary School

A team involving several families, together with their children, worked hard in producing relevant scripts to aid the school curriculum. They were excitedly welcomed at our local school for their termly visits.

There were whole church productions such as "Angels Aware" and "The Lion, the Witch and the Wardrobe" whose performances were avidly attended by many visitors and friends from the village, which also included the puppet ministry. The school's ministry itself expanded over a number of years to include visits to a variety of schools in the Maidstone area.

It was a real joy for me to attend many of these assembly opportunities, and to observe how the gospel could be well communicated to children and staff alike in a most acceptable way with real joy and excitement.

Churches Together in Staplehurst (CTiS)

For many years the churches in this village have worked together in a variety of ways to share the opportunities to witness to Christ in our community. When I first came to the village the Catholic community met in "The Convent of the Good Shepherd", on the outskirts of the village, but after a number of years the convent was closed and many of their congregation moved to various Catholic churches in Goudhurst, Cranbrook and Benenden. Other churches in the village include All Saints Anglican church, and Staplehurst United Reformed Church, both in the High Street, the Strict Baptist church in Chapel Lane, as well as the Free Church in Station Road.

We have a united committee made up of three lay persons from each church, if at all possible, and clergy from each church are invited each time we meet, normally about six times a year. With my heart to see churches working together, supporting one another in promoting Kingdom truths to the community, I have been a regular attender at these meetings for the whole time of our presence in the village. It has been a real joy to serve alongside Christians from each of the different congregations.

Lynne has recently joined our committee too. Our activities include producing Christmas and Easter cards that are delivered by volunteers to every house in the village. We regularly hold united services in one another's churches, and always celebrate together the "Week of Prayer for Christian Unity", in January each year. What formerly was the "Women's World Day of Prayer" in March, but is now known simply as "The World Day of Prayer", to which men are also invited, is arranged by our group as well. Before I arrived in the village a united Alpha Course was organised, which proved a great success, although such events are now generally organised by individual churches.

During the lockdown for the Covid-19 Pandemic which struck the world and our nation in 2020/21, I was privileged to conduct two online Alpha courses. It included a number of people from our village, but also from further afield including Headcorn, Maidstone, Lincolnshire and Scotland!

In 2006 the churches worked together on a united mission in our local park in Surrenden Field where we pitched a large marquee for a week of outreach meetings entitled,

"Celebration of Life", which included visits from the Bishop of Maidstone, my prayer partner Rob Frost the Methodist evangelist, Fiona Castle, the wife of the late entertainer Roy Castle, "Tough Talk", a group of Christian strong men, and various children's evangelists. We put together a team of full-time workers for the week, made up of local Christians from the village, and those from outside the community who felt the Lord call them to join us.

"Celebration of Life" - a parachute game on Surrenden Field

The team all wore green t-shirts, as we joined lots of children who attended from the school for a parachute game. It was a wonderful week of Christian unity affecting the whole village, which culminated in a joint celebration on the Sunday to which Graham Cray, the Bishop of Maidstone, came to address the gathered crowd of villagers.

There is something special about this village, where churches are prepared to live and work together, forgetting any differences and uniting in our common goal to preach the good news of Jesus! It was a most successful time where people were encouraged in their faith as they served the community together. Some came to faith in Christ for the first time, and the village certainly knew that the churches could work together to good effect. One comment made by one of our villagers was that "You know that God is on the move when you see churches working together!"

The churches gladly financed the project together so that we didn't need to make any appeals and the local school was delighted to arrange a timetable for each class to attend an activity suitable to their age group. "Psarms Puppets" were also able to be involved. There were ladies' groups, youth meetings, children's entertainers, evening outreach events, a prayer labyrinth, prayer times and worship times. We were delighted to serve the Lord and the community in this way. I was thrilled to be involved and to see the Lord moving in so many lives as we endeavoured to honour Him.

Rob Frost preaching in the marquee at an evening meeting

Community Fridge

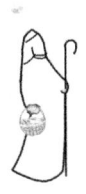

THE SHEPHERD'S PANTRY

COMMUNITY FRIDGE

Save on food bills & help prevent food waste

A selection of donated and shop surplus food available to anyone, for free

In recent years, since coming out of lockdown, we as a church have been guided by the Lord to open a community fridge. We are able to pass on to those who may be in need, a variety of food products as they reach their sell by date, given to us by local shops, individuals and supermarkets.

A whole group of volunteers from the church formed a rota so we were able to open four days a week. We were amazed how many individuals and families took up the offer, and have been really encouraged by the number of people who, not only come to collect groceries, but also stay for a drink and a chat.

What has also been thrilling is to see the numbers of village people who don't necessarily attend our services, but want to volunteer in a whole variety of ways. This might include such things as manning the centre, collecting produce from the supermarkets and sorting the food stuffs as they arrive, establishing what needs to be given away straight away and what might be kept for a while longer.

Associated with this has been the "Warm Hub". Over the winter of 2022/23 the government encouraged voluntary bodies to set up centres where people could come to sit, chat and keep warm, due to the fuel crisis across the nation. A number of centres were set up in Staplehurst so that, if necessary, people could visit one each day to keep warm, cutting down on the heating bills at home. Our centre opened each Tuesday from 12:30 to 4:00pm and attracted some 20 to 40 people each week. When the spring arrived, those participants had so enjoyed meeting and sharing with one another, that they asked whether it was possible for the Warm Hub to continue indefinitely, and so it does even to this day!

The Emmaus Project

In 1987 I was involved with Rob Frost, my prayer partner, in Mission '87', and was asked to lead an evangelistic mission to a village in Yorkshire. I visited the church and congregation six months beforehand to attend a meeting of their leaders and members. They asked me what I was going to do, to help them "do" evangelism, but I replied that I was coming **alongside** to help them achieve whatever was in their hearts, in order to reach their neighbours and community. Over the following months they put in place a variety of outreach events which I, together with the team allotted to me, slotted into, in order to help them accomplish their goals.

In the Summer of 2022, the leadership at SFC began to sense they were directed to a ministry known as the "Emmaus Project", which interestingly was being implemented by "Share Jesus International" (SJI) a ministry founded by Rob Frost, and whose son Andy, is the present CEO. He himself, has ministered at SFC in a preaching/teaching capacity several times in recent years, and I had the privilege of mentoring him in his early years in his role as CEO. The leadership commended to the church that we become part of this project to aid the church in our outreach ministry in the following two years. For over 20 years, SJI has been working with local churches to encourage people to share their faith in Jesus. Over that time, they have created courses, toured events, hosted training days and led missions that have served countless churches across the UK.

"The Emmaus project" is about offering more than resources and pre-packaged events. SJI work **alongside** local churches to help embed faith sharing into all that they do. They have found that when churches have an external viewpoint from a seasoned evangelist, they give a unique perspective that helps the local church become more effective in sharing Jesus.

The tailored two-year programme includes:

• A stocktake of where things are at within the church, and our outreach potential
• A prayerful exploration of what sustainable mission in the community could look like
• Regular training for the congregation
• Preaching two to three times a year on relevant themes
• Regular phone or Zoom calls with the church leaders, and person to person sessions with our leadership team

The evangelists who we were privileged to have serve alongside us were Andy Frost and Marcus Bennett. Their mini-biographies are offered below:

Andy Frost has been the Director of "Share Jesus International" since 2008, leading scores of projects ranging from London's Pentecost Festival to national tours. At the heart of all that he does, he wants to help people follow Jesus. He is a popular speaker who loves telling the stories of Jesus. He presently heads up the London Mission Collective; works with "Care for the Family" on the Kitchen Table Project and "Gather" on church unity and mission.

Over the years he has worked with a variety of organisations including "More than Gold", "Big Book Media" and "C3 Global". He is a Methodist Local Preacher, has an MA in Applied Theology, and has authored a number of books, and presented the "Jesus Series".

He is married to Jo and has two daughters. His downtime is spent watching live comedy, playing football or searching for waves to surf.

Marcus has been in ministry for 25 years, leading local churches, church planting, training and equipping churches for evangelism and community engagement.

He is passionate about the church escaping its walls and making a difference within the local community. Some of his projects have included, helping to establish Wimbledon Foodbank and the first daytime Street Angels in Dewsbury.

He started his evangelism journey as a student and a new Christian in the early 90s with the forerunner to SJI, so is delighted to be returning as a trainer.

He is married to Sue, a singer and vocal coach and has two musical daughters, although his only musical talents are being roadie and audience.

Over the two years we have had a number of evangelistic events, which include barn dances, quiz nights and special outreach events at Christmas and Easter, all of which have seen packed audiences. We have held practical seminars on ways to share our faith and helped to see the importance of well-planned and thought through events with good follow up procedures in place.

All in all, it has proved to be a fruitful time for the Kingdom culminating recently in a baptismal service for five candidates. Already several others are asking for baptism later in the year. The Bennett family have served us by holding two musical concert evenings with Sue, Faith and Grace providing the music and song, while Marcus entertained the audiences with his gifted story telling.

Present Ministry At Staplehurst Free Church

We as a church had been involved in an interregnum for a number of years and felt it right in 2023 to contact various ministries, church friends and contacts to pray with us, as we sought another person to become our church pastoral leader.

Two years previously, a couple came to join our church, together with their two teenage sons. Peter, Alison, Finlay and Cameron, soon became a valuable asset to the church.

Peter, Alison, Finlay and Cameron Brook

Interestingly Alison had spent some time in the youth group of the church in her teenage years, but now with her musical talent, became a great contributor to the church worship group. Peter, when completing university had felt a call to ministry, but for a variety of reasons nothing seemed to open up for him in that direction, so followed a career in the secular world while still being involved in church voluntary work, and as a leader in a variety of churches throughout his life.

After a year or so with us, Peter was invited to become an elder of the church, and when we put out our feelers to others about a possible pastoral/leader, he asked to be considered. This, for me, was a return to the principle of God raising up leaders from the church, which I had envisioned over the years and so, thoroughly excited me.

After a period of consultation with the leadership, the congregation and his family, Peter was invited to become a part-time pastoral church leader for Staplehurst Free Church. He took up the role in December 2023 and has been doing an excellent job. The story of our church in Staplehurst is to be continued!

Final Thoughts

For me, I have so many other things I could perhaps include or allude to in these writings, but feel I have done sufficient to fulfil that initial suggestion from the Hospital Chaplain back in 2022, that I have sensed was an invitation from the Lord.

I found this Bible verse this week in my daily devotions. This, I believe, is a fitting place to finish. To God be the glory!

Many, LORD my God, are the wonders you have done, the things you planned for us. None can compare with you; were I to speak and tell of your deeds, they would be too many to declare. (Psalm 40:5 NIV)

Clive Jones, August 2024

The Jones Family

Back Row: Naomi's Mum, Clair, Sam, Naomi's
brother, Martyn, Naomi, Naomi's Dad
Front Row: Clive, Lylah, Lynne and Malia
at Malia's dedication at SFC, 5th October 2014

Lylah and Clair

August 2024 - Lylah aged 13 excited to be standing outside Voisons in St Helier, Jersey where her great grandfather worked

Naomi, Malia, Leo and Martyn

Clive and Lynne

Malia and Leo, January 2024

Clive, Clair, Lynne, Lylah, Malia, Martyn and
Naomi in 2016

Clive and Phyllis at Scotney Castle

May the Lord Jesus Christ and God our Father (who has loved us and given us unending encouragement and unfailing hope by His grace) inspire YOU with courage and confidence in every good thing you say or do.

2 Thessalonians 2:16-17
(JB Phillips Translation)

Printed in Great Britain
by Amazon